STEP·BY

ENGLISH
Cooking

Your Promise of Success

Welcome to the world of Confident Cooking, created for you in our
Test Kitchen, where recipes are double–tested by our team
of home economists to achieve a high standard of success.

MURDOCH BOOKS®
Sydney • London • Vancouver

BASIC ENGLISH PANTRY

Apart from the staples, such as flour, sugar and eggs, these are some of the ingredients which make English cooking unique.

Apple cider: Made from fermented apples, it may be alcoholic or non–alcoholic. Apple juice may be substituted.

Bain marie: A water bath used to keep foods at below boiling point to prevent spoiling or overcooking. A large baking dish can be used for this purpose.

Bay leaf: The leaf of an evergreen laurel tree. Used as a flavouring in stews, casseroles and soups.

Black treacle: Black, viscous, uncrystallised syrup obtained from refined sugar. It is darker and stronger in flavouring than golden syrup, and is similar to molasses.

Chantilly cream: Whipped cream which is sweetened with sugar or icing sugar and flavoured with vanilla.

Demerara sugar: A white sugar treated with molasses to produce a pale golden sugar. The size of the crystal is larger than white sugar.

Dripping: A fat made from rendered beef or sheep; can be purchased in solid blocks from the supermarket or butcher.

Dry mustard: Mustard powder made from ground, yellow mustard seeds. English dry mustard powder is hot, so use sparingly.

Forequarter chops: Lamb chops cut from the front legs of the lamb. Bone forms a large part of the weight.

Gammon: The hind of a cured side of bacon, used for ham and ham steaks.

Golden syrup: A light-coloured treacle manufactured from crystalline sugar.

Haddock: Usually smoked and known as Finnan Haddock. Haddock is a North Atlantic fish with a firm flesh. If not available, substitute smoked cod.

Horseradish: Root of the horseradish plant. Commercially made horseradish is a mixture of grated horseradish root, oil, vinegar and sugar.

Knead: To knead the dough, bring the edges to the centre and then push it outwards with the knuckles of the folded hand. The kneading process helps to blend the ingredients and

develop the gluten which contributes to the structure and grain of the finished product.

Lard: Soft, white, odourless rendered pig fat used as a shortening agent. It can be used in pies, cakes or biscuits or used as a frying medium.

Malt vinegar: Made from malted barley, fermented, and coloured with caramel. It is used mainly for pickling and in worcestershire sauce.

Mace: A spice from the outer casing of the nutmeg. It has a similar taste to nutmeg, but is stronger and is usually ground to a fine powder.

Oatmeal: This is produced from ground oats, and can be purchased from health food shops. It comes in three grades: coarse, medium and fine.

Prunes: The purplish-black dried fruit of several plum varieties. They are a rich source of vitamin A.

Puff pastry: There are three different types: ready–rolled sheets, ready–rolled butter puff and pastry in a block, which has to be rolled out. The butter pastry has a higher fat content and richer flavour.

Sage: A herb used alone or blended with thyme and marjoram to form the traditional mixed herbs. Sage counteracts the richness in foods while at the same time helping the digestion.

Suet: Unprocessed fat from around a cow's kidney. It is grated and used as a shortening in puddings, pastries and pies, to make them rich and moist. It can be obtained fresh from a butcher. A dehydrated form is available from the supermarket.

Worcestershire sauce: Commercially bottled English-style sauce made with soya beans, garlic, anchovies, tamarind, onion, spices and malt vinegar.

Yeast: A living organism used as a raising agent in breads and doughs, yeast is available either fresh (compressed) or dried. Fresh yeast is sold at health food stores and delicatessens, and keeps up to three days in the refrigerator.

3

Add chopped butter to flour and sugar, rub in with fingertips.

Roll dough out into rectangle 35 cm long x 22 cm wide.

Spread dough with butter, sprinkle with sugar and mixed fruit.

Remove glaze from heat and brush over cooked bun.

TEATIME

A cup of tea, complete with scones, a cake or buns, is a delightful ritual of English life.

Chelsea Buns

A sweet, sticky treat.

Preparation time:
35 minutes
Total cooking time:
25–30 minutes
Serves 8

---

*2 cups self-raising
flour
1/4 cup caster sugar
30 g butter, chopped
1/3 cup milk
1 egg*

*FILLING
30 g butter, softened
1 tablespoon soft
brown sugar
1 cup dried mixed
fruit
1 teaspoon ground
mixed spice*

*GLAZE
1/4 cup sugar
1/4 cup water*

---

1 Preheat oven to moderately hot 210°C (190°C gas). Brush a 20 cm square cake tin with melted butter or oil. Line base of tin with baking paper. Sift flour and sugar into a bowl, add chopped butter. Using your fingertips, rub butter into flour until the mixture is fine and crumbly.

2 Whisk milk and egg together, pour onto sifted ingredients and mix to form a soft dough. Turn onto a sheet of baking paper and roll into a rectangle 35 cm long x 22 cm wide.

3 Spread dough with softened butter, sprinkle with sugar, mixed fruit and mixed spice. Roll up; cut into 12 even-sized pieces. Place cut side down in prepared tin with sides touching. Reduce oven to moderate 180°C. Bake 25–30 minutes until brown and cooked through. Remove; place on wire cooling rack.

4 To make Glaze: Place sugar and water into a small pan. Stir over medium heat without boiling until sugar dissolves. Bring to the boil for 2–3 minutes. Remove from heat and brush over buns. To serve, split and butter.

HINT
If you're short of time, use a food processor to combine butter and flour, then add egg and milk and process until mixture holds together.

Devonshire Scones

Preparation time:
15 minutes
Total cooking time:
15–20 minutes
Makes 15

3 cups self-raising flour	*beaten egg for glaze*
2 tablespoons sugar	
50 g butter, chopped	*strawberry jam and whipped cream to serve*
1 cup milk	

1 Preheat oven to moderately hot 210°C (190°C gas). Brush a flat baking tray with melted butter or oil. Sift flour into a large mixing bowl, add sugar. Using your fingertips, rub through butter until mixture resembles fine breadcrumbs.

2 Make a well in the centre and pour in milk, mix to form a soft, slightly sticky dough.

3 Turn onto a floured surface and knead lightly. Pat or roll to a 2 cm thickness. Cut into 6 cm rounds with scone or biscuit cutter and place close together onto the prepared tray.

4 Brush with beaten egg. Bake for 15–20 minutes. Serve hot with jam and cream.

Using fingertips, rub butter into sifted flour and sugar.

Pour in milk, mix to form a soft, slightly sticky dough.

Cut dough into 6 cm rounds with scone or biscuit cutter.

Place rounds on prepared tray, brush with beaten egg.

Pikelets

Quick and easy.

Preparation time:
10 minutes
Total cooking time:
15 minutes
Makes 16 pikelets

---

1 cup *self-raising flour*
2 tablespoons *sugar*
1/4 teaspoon
   bicarbonate of soda
1/2–3/4 cup *milk*

1/2 teaspoon *lemon
   juice or vinegar*
1 egg, *lightly beaten*
30 g butter, *melted*
extra melted butter

---

1 Sift flour, sugar and soda into a medium size mixing bowl. Add juice or vinegar to the milk to sour it; allow to stand 5 minutes.
2 Make well in centre of dry ingredients and add the egg, 1/2 cup milk and the butter; mix to form a smooth batter. If batter is too thick to pour from the spoon, add remaining milk.

3 Brush base of frying pan lightly with melted butter. Drop 1–2 tablespoons of mixture onto base of pan about 2 cm apart. Cook over medium heat 1 minute or until underside is golden.
4 Turn over and cook other side. Remove from pan; repeat with remaining mixture. Serve warm with butter pat or curls.

Add lemon juice to milk and let stand 5 minutes to sour it.

Pour egg, milk and butter into well in dry ingredients.

Drop tablespoons of mixture onto base of pan, 2 cm apart.

Turn browned pikelets over and cook other side.

Lincolnshire Plum Bread

Preparation time:
20 minutes
Total cooking time:
1 hour 15 minutes
Makes 1 loaf

---

150 g prunes,
roughly chopped
1/4 cup boiling water
2 tablespoons brandy
125 g butter
1/2 cup caster sugar
1 tablespoon black
treacle
2 eggs, lightly beaten
3/4 cup currants

2/3 cup sultanas
1 1/2 cups self-raising
flour
3/4 teaspoon cinnamon
1/2 teaspoon mixed
spice
1/4 teaspoon salt
icing sugar, for
dusting

---

1 Preheat oven to slow 150°C. Brush a 21 x 14 x 7 cm loaf tin with melted butter or oil; line base with baking paper. Place prunes in a small bowl and cover with water and brandy. Set aside to soak for 10 minutes.

2 Using electric beaters, beat butter and sugar in a small mixing bowl until light and creamy. Add treacle; mix well. Add eggs gradually, beating well after each addition. The mixture will appear slightly curdled at this stage, but this is to be expected.

3 Transfer mixture to a large mixing bowl. Add fruit, including liquid from soaking prunes.

4 Using a metal spoon, fold in sifted flour, spices and salt. Spoon into prepared tin, smooth surface with a flat-bladed knife. Bake for 1 hour 15 minutes or until skewer comes out clean when inserted into centre of the bread. Leave to stand in tin for 10 minutes before turning out onto wire rack to cool. Dust the loaf with sifted icing sugar before serving.

Cover prunes with water and brandy, soak for 10 minutes.

Cream butter and sugar, add treacle and mix well.

Add fruit, including liquid from soaking prunes, to mixture.

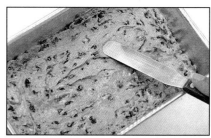

Spoon mixture into tin, smooth surface with flat-bladed knife.

11

Lardy Cake

Be sure to use pork lard for this recipe.

Preparation time:
2 hours (includes proving time)
Total cooking time:
45 minutes
Makes one 20cm square cake

---

2 x 7 g sachets dried yeast
1 teaspoon sugar
1 cup warm water
3 cups plain flour
1 teaspoon ground cinnamon

60 g lard
1/3 cup currants
2 tablespoons soft brown sugar
1 egg, lightly beaten
2 teaspoons demerara sugar

---

1 Brush a 20 cm square tin with melted butter or oil. Line base with baking paper. Combine yeast, sugar and water in a small bowl. Cover with plastic wrap and set aside in a warm place for 15 minutes or until the liquid becomes frothy on the surface.
2 Sift flour and cinnamon into a large bowl. Make a well in the centre, add yeast mixture. Using a knife, mix to a soft dough. Turn onto a lightly floured surface, knead for 10 minutes until smooth and elastic. Shape dough into a ball, place in a large, lightly oiled bowl. Leave covered with plastic wrap in a warm place for 1 hour or until doubled in size.
3 Preheat oven to moderately hot 210°C (190°C gas). Punch air out of dough and turn onto a lightly floured surface. Knead for 1 minute, then roll into a rectangle 30 x 20 cm. Place half the lard over the top two-thirds of the dough in small pats, sprinkle with half the currants and half the brown sugar. Fold dough into three layers. Press edges together, give a quarter turn.
4 Roll out dough again and repeat with remaining filling. Fold pastry into three layers, then roll lightly to form a 20 x 20 cm square. Place into prepared tin, cover with plastic wrap and leave for 20 minutes to rise. Brush with beaten egg, sprinkle with demerara sugar, and bake for 45 minutes until golden.
Note: A traditional English recipe, Lardy Cake is served cold cut into slices with or without butter. Although lard is not often used by modern health-conscious cooks, no other fat can be substituted in this recipe.

Set yeast mixture aside until it is frothy on the surface.

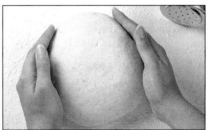

Knead dough for 10 minutes, then shape into a ball.

Sprinkle dough rectangle with half lard, currants and sugar.

Sprinkle dough with demerara sugar, bake until golden.

Eccles Cakes

Not too sweet.

Preparation time:
20 minutes
Total cooking time:
15–20 minutes
Makes 27

---

1 cup currants
1/2 cup mixed peel
1 tablespoon brandy
1 tablespoon sugar
1/2 teaspoon ground
  cinnamon

3 sheets ready-rolled
  butter puff pastry
1 egg white
2 teaspoons sugar,
  extra

---

1 Preheat oven to moderately hot 210°C (190°C gas). Brush two oven trays with melted butter. Combine currants, peel, brandy, sugar and cinnamon in bowl.
2 Using a scone cutter, cut nine 8 cm circles from each sheet of pastry. Place two level teaspoons of filling on each circle.

3 Bring edges of circles together and pinch to seal. Turn seam side down, roll out to 1 cm-thick oval.
4 Place on trays. Brush tops of cakes with egg white and sprinkle with extra sugar. With a knife, make three slashes across top of each cake. Bake for 15–20 minutes, until golden.

Combine currants, peel, brandy, sugar and cinnamon in bowl.

Place 2 level teaspoons of filling on each pastry circle.

Turn filled pastry seam side down, roll out to oval shape.

Using a sharp knife, score tops of cakes with three slashes.

Rub surface of meat with mustard, pepper and salt.

Place meat in a baking dish, fat side up.

MEAT, FISH & POULTRY

Main course meals are hearty and nourishing, having been evolved over the years to suit the colder climate.

Roast Beef with Yorkshire Pudding

Preparation time:
15 minutes
Total cooking time:
1½–2 hours
Serves 6

2 kg piece of sirloin on the bone	**YORKSHIRE PUDDING**
½ teaspoon dry mustard	**¾ cup plain flour**
½ teaspoon ground black pepper	**salt, to taste**
salt to taste	**1 egg, lightly beaten**
60 g dripping or oil	**¼ cup water**
	½ cup milk
	30 g dripping or butter, melted

1 Preheat oven to moderate 180°C. Trim meat, score the fat, rub surface with mustard, pepper and salt. Heat dripping in frying pan until hot; quickly seal the meat, fat side down. Brown all sides.

2 Place meat in a baking dish, fat side up. Roast 25–30 minutes per 500 g for medium roast beef. Stand 15 minutes before carving.

3 For Pudding: Sift flour and salt into bowl, add combined egg and water. Mix to paste. Heat milk and pour in, beat until smooth. Pour dripping into 12-cup deep patty tray. Heat in 210°C oven 5 minutes. Divide batter between cups, bake for 10-15 minutes or until puffed.

Alternative batter:
1 cup self-raising flour, 4 eggs, 1 cup milk, 1 cup water.
Follow method above.

Heat milk and pour into batter, beat until smooth.

Divide batter evenly between the cups in patty tray.

Bangers and Mash

Preparation time:
  25 minutes
Total cooking time:
  25 minutes
Serves 4

---

1 tablespoon oil	*4 medium potatoes*
8 thick sausages	*2 tablespoons milk*
2 medium onions, sliced	*30 g butter*
2 tablespoons gravy powder	*salt and pepper*
1½ cups water	*finely chopped parsley, for garnish*

1 Prick the sausages with a fork. Heat oil in a large heavy-based frying pan; add sausages. Cook over a medium heat for 10 minutes, until they are brown and cooked through. Transfer sausages to a plate covered with paper towel.

2 Pour off most of the fat from pan, leaving about a tablespoon. Add onions and cook over a medium heat for 5 minutes until soft and golden.

3 Combine gravy powder with water in a jug, stir until smooth. Add to pan, stir to combine with onions. Stir gravy constantly over a medium low heat for 2 minutes or until mixture boils and thickens. Return sausages to pan. Combine with gravy and serve immediately with mash.

4 To make Mash: Cook potatoes in a large pan of boiling water until tender; drain well. Mash with a potato masher until free from lumps. Add milk and butter, blend with a fork until smooth and creamy. Add salt and pepper to taste. Sprinkle chopped parsley over potatoes to serve.

Note: Bangers and Mash may be served with a green vegetable, such as beans or peas.

Peel and slice onions, prick sausages with a fork.

Cook onions about 5 minutes or until soft and golden.

Return cooked sausages to pan with onions and gravy.

Add milk and butter to potatoes, blend until smooth and creamy.

19

Oxtail Soup

A meal in one.

Preparation time:
10 minutes
Total cooking time:
3 hours
Makes 4 litres

---

*1 oxtail
(approx 750 g)*
30 g butter
*1 large parsnip,
peeled and finely
chopped*
*1 turnip, peeled and
finely chopped*
*2 large carrots,
peeled and finely
chopped*
*2 sticks celery, finely
chopped*

*1 large onion, finely
chopped*
*2 tablespoons
barley*
4 whole cloves
*1/4 cup chopped
parsley*
8 cups stock
white pepper
salt to taste

---

1 Trim oxtail and cut into 2.5 cm pieces.
2 Melt butter in a large heavy-based pan. Add oxtail in batches. Cook until browned; remove and drain. Add parsnip, turnip, carrots, celery and onion; stir until onion becomes transparent.
3 Return meat to pan. Add barley, cloves, parsley, stock, pepper and salt.
4 Simmer for 2½ hours, skimming the froth off the surface as it rises in the pan. Serve in individual soup bowls, accompanied by bread or toast.
Note: Oxtail Soup is very filling, and is generally served as a main course or as a hearty lunch.

HINT

If you are buying oxtail prepackaged from the supermarket, choose the larger pieces, cut from the top of the tail. They will be meatier and have more flavour.
In the past, a mixture of oxtail and oxcheek was used for making oxtail soup.

Trim oxtail of fat and cut it into 2.5 cm pieces.

Cook in heavy-based pan in batches until browned; remove and drain.

Add parsley to all other ingredients in the pan.

Simmer 2½ hours, skimming the surface

Devilled Kidneys

Good as a starter.

Preparation time:
10 minutes
Total cooking time:
30 minutes
Serves 4

---

8 lamb kidneys	*1 tablespoon*
60 g butter	*worcestershire sauce*
1 medium onion,	*1 tablespoon tomato*
finely chopped	*sauce*
1 teaspoon dry	*1½ cups stock*
mustard	*salt to taste*
¼ cup plain flour	*toast fingers to serve*

1 Remove fine skin membrane and core from kidneys. Cut into 5 mm slices.
2 Heat butter in a heavy-based frying pan. Add onion and cook until onion just changes colour. Add kidneys and brown. Reduce heat to simmer; remove kidneys and set aside.

3 Sprinkle mustard and flour over base of pan and cook, stirring, until flour is golden brown.
4 Add sauces, stock and salt and stir until mixture comes to boil; reduce heat, simmer 5 minutes. Add kidneys to sauce, cook 15 minutes over low heat. Serve with toast.

Remove fine skin membrane and core from kidneys, cut into slices.

Add kidneys to onion in frying pan and brown all over.

Sprinkle dry mustard and flour over cooked onions in base of pan.

Add sauces, stock and salt to pan, stir until mixture is smooth.

Rabbit Stew with Dumplings

Preparation time:
15 minutes
Total cooking time:
1 hour 15 minutes
Serves 6–8

---

*2 large rabbits
(2 kg)
1/3 cup plain flour
1/2 teaspoon dry
mustard
50 g butter
1 large brown onion,
finely chopped
2 sticks celery, thinly
sliced
2 carrots, peeled and
thinly sliced
2 1/2 cups dry apple
cider
1/2 teaspoon ground
mace*

*ground black pepper
salt to taste
1 bay leaf*

*DUMPLINGS
1 cup self-raising
flour
20 g dripping
1 tablespoon chopped
fresh parsley
1/4 cup cider or water
chopped parsley for
garnish*

---

1 Preheat oven to moderate 180°C. Brush a 6-cup capacity heatproof dish with melted butter or oil. Cut each rabbit into eight pieces. Combine flour and mustard on a sheet of greaseproof paper. Toss rabbit in flour; shake off excess. Reserve the remaining flour and mustard mixture.

2 Melt butter in frying pan. Add rabbit, cook over medium heat on all sides until brown. Place in prepared dish. Add onion, celery and carrot to pan; cook until onion softens. Remove from heat and scatter over rabbit. Sprinkle reserved flour over pan and cook until brown. Pour over cider and stir until the mixture comes to the boil and thickens. Season with mace, pepper and salt. Add bay leaf. Pour sauce over rabbit and vegetables. Bake, covered, for 1 hour.

3 To make Dumplings: Sift flour into a medium bowl. Add dripping and parsley. Mix with sufficient water or cider to a firm dough.

4 Shape into six or eight tiny dumplings and place on top of rabbit stew. Cook, covered, for a further 15 minutes. Serve sprinkled with additional chopped parsley.

Note: Rabbits may be obtained from a butcher or a game specialist. They need long, slow cooking, until the meat is literally falling from the bone, as they have a tendency to be tough.

Cut rabbit into eight serving-sized pieces.

Cook onion, celery and carrot and scatter over rabbit in dish.

Mix flour, dripping and parsley with water or cider to form dough.

Shape tiny dumplings and place on top of rabbit stew.

25

Oxford Sausages

Skinless and easy.

Preparation time:
15 minutes
Total cooking time:
20 minutes
Serves 4

8 slices white bread,
    crusts removed
750 g pork and veal
    mince
2 teaspoons finely
    grated lemon rind

1/4 cup lemon juice
1 teaspoon dried sage
1/2 teaspoon cracked
    black pepper
salt to taste

1 Preheat oven to moderately hot 210°C (190°C gas). Brush a baking tray with melted butter or oil.

Remove crusts from bread, tear each slice into large pieces and place in a food processor bowl.

Using the pulse action, press button for 20 seconds, until large crumbs form.
2 Place all ingredients in a large mixing bowl. Using hands, combine thoroughly.
3 Divide mixture into eight portions. With wet hands, form into 13 cm-long log shapes.
4 Place sausages on prepared tray. Bake for 20 minutes, until browned. Serve with toast.

Using pulse action, process white bread until large crumbs form.

In a large bowl, mix all ingredients thoroughly, using your hands.

Form mixture into eight log shapes, approximately 13 cm long.

Place sausages on tray and bake for 20 minutes, until brown.

Lancashire Hot Pot

Preparation time:
20 minutes
Total cooking time:
2 hours
Serves 8

---

8 forequarter chops,
cut 2.5 cm thick
50 g dripping or
butter
1/4 cup plain flour
2 large brown onions,
sliced
2 sticks celery,
chopped
1 large parsnip,
peeled and sliced
1¾ cups chicken or
beef stock

200 g mushrooms,
sliced
1/2 teaspoon white
pepper
salt to taste
2 teaspoons dried
mixed herbs
1 tablespoon
worcestershire
sauce
4 medium old
potatoes, thinly
sliced

---

1 Preheat oven to moderately slow 160°C. Brush a large 6-cup capacity heatproof casserole dish, with lid, with melted butter or oil. Trim meat of excess fat and sinew. Heat dripping in a large frying pan; toss chops in flour. Shake off excess and fry chops quickly either side until brown. Remove chops and place in casserole dish.

2 Add onions, celery and parsnip to pan, cook until parsnip is coloured. Place mixture on top of chops.

3 Sprinkle remaining flour over base of pan and cook, stirring, until dark brown. Gradually pour in stock and stir until mixture comes to the boil. Add mushrooms, pepper, salt, herbs and worcestershire sauce, simmer for 10 minutes. Remove from heat and pour over chops.

4 Place overlapping slices of potato to completely cover the meat and vegetables. Cover casserole dish with lid and place into preheated oven. Cook for 1¼ hours. Remove lid and continue cooking for a further 30 minutes or until potatoes are brown.

Note: Lancashire Hot Pot is the English version of Irish Stew. It is customarily served with pickled red cabbage, a traditional dish throughout Northern Europe which goes by different names in different countries. Basically, it is finely sliced cabbage which is packed into a storage jar with layers of salt. Bay leaves and peppercorns are added and the cabbage is left to mature for four weeks before using.

Trim chops, toss in flour and shake off excess.

Slice onions and parsnip, chop celery and add to pan.

Add mushrooms, pepper, salt, herbs and worcestershire sauce.

Place overlapping slices of potato over meat and vegetables.

Kedgeree

A breakfast dish.

Preparation time:
15 minutes
Total cooking time:
30 minutes
Serves 4

500 g smoked
  haddock
1 teaspoon finely
  grated lemon rind
1 bay leaf
250 g (1½ cups)
  cooked long
  grain rice
3 hard-boiled eggs,
  finely chopped

¼ teaspoon ground
  nutmeg
pinch pepper
salt to taste
1 tablespoon lemon
  juice
50 g butter, chopped
¾ cup cream

1 Preheat oven to moderate 180°C. Brush a shallow 6-cup capacity ovenproof dish with melted butter or oil. Cut fish into 3 cm cubes, place in large pan with lemon rind and bay leaf, cover with water and simmer until just cooked, about 6–8 minutes.
2 Using a slotted spoon, remove fish pieces from liquid. Flake fish with a fork.
3 In a large bowl, combine cooked rice, eggs, fish, nutmeg, pepper, salt and lemon juice.
4 Spoon mixture into prepared dish. Dot the top of the kedgeree with butter, pour over cream. Bake for 20 minutes. Serve with buttered toast and lemon slices.

HINT
Kedgeree takes its name from Khichri, an Indian rice and lentil dish, adapted by the English in the days of the Raj. It is sometimes made with leftover fish, but make sure that there is a good proportion of fish to rice, so that it is not stodgy, and use plenty of butter and cream. It is particularly good made with a fish such as salmon.

Place fish in frying pan with lemon rind and bayleaf.

Remove fish from cooking liquid and flake with a fork.

Combine rice, eggs, fish, nutmeg, pepper, salt and juice.

Spoon mixture into dish and dot the top with butter.

Fish and Chips

Traditionally served with vinegar and plenty of salt.

Preparation time:
15 minutes
+ 10 minutes
standing
Total cooking time:
30 minutes
Serves 6

BATTER
1½ cups plain flour
½ cup self-raising flour
salt to taste
⅔ cup water
¾ cup milk
1 egg, lightly beaten

2 tablespoons white vinegar

1 kg white fish fillets
5 large old potatoes
2 lemons
oil for deep frying

---

1 To make Batter: Sift flours and salt into large bowl. Make a well in the centre. In jug, whisk together water, milk, egg and vinegar. Gradually pour liquid mixture into well in flours. Mix with a wooden spoon to form a smooth batter; stand 10 minutes before using.

2 Trim fish, removing any skin and/or bones; trim into serving-sized pieces. Peel potatoes and cut into 1 cm slices, then into chip lengths 1 cm wide. Place potatoes into water until ready to use.

3 Heat oil in deep pan. Drain and dry potato chips with paper towel. Gently lower chips a few at a time into moderately hot oil. Cook over medium heat 4 minutes or until pale golden. Drain well on paper towel. Before serving, reheat oil; cook chips again in batches until crisp and golden. Drain and serve with fish.

4 Reduce oil temperature. Dip fish into batter, coat evenly. Deep-fry 4–5 minutes until batter is crisp and golden. Drain on paper towel.

Make well in centre of flour and pour in liquids.

Cut peeled potatoes into 1 cm-thick slices, then into chip lengths.

Gently lower chips, a few at a time, into moderately hot oil.

Deep-fry fish until it is cooked, and batter is crisp.

Chicken Pudding

Warming for winter.

Preparation time:
20 minutes
Total cooking time:
1 hour
Serves 6

---

1 kg chicken thigh
    fillets
3 sticks celery,
    chopped
1 large brown onion,
    finely chopped
2 bay leaves
3 cups chicken stock

1 cup self-raising
    flour
1/2 teaspoon black
    pepper
salt to taste
1 teaspoon ground
    mace
30 g butter, melted
1 egg, lightly beaten

---

1 Grease a shallow heatproof dish with melted butter or oil; preheat oven to 180°C. Trim chicken fillets of excess fat and sinew and cut each into three pieces. Place chicken, celery, onion, bay leaves and chicken stock into a deep pan. Bring to the boil, reduce heat and simmer gently for 10 minutes or until chicken is just cooked. Discard bay leaves.

2 Remove chicken, celery and onion from pan and place into prepared heatproof dish. Reserve two cups of liquid for pudding batter – allow it to cool before using. Discard remaining liquid.

3 Sift flour, pepper, salt and mace into a large bowl. Make a well in the centre. Whisk together melted butter, egg and reserved liquid. Pour the liquid mixture over the sifted ingredients and beat with a wooden spoon to a smooth batter.

4 Pour mixture over chicken pieces. Bake in preheated oven for 30–45 minutes until top is set and golden brown. Serve hot with vegetables in season.

Trim thigh fillets of fat and sinew; cut each into three pieces.

Place chicken, celery and onion into heatproof dish.

Stir butter, egg and reserved liquid into dry ingredients.

Beat to a smooth batter and pour over chicken pieces.

Toad in the Hole

Easy and delicious.

Preparation time:
  25 minutes
Total cooking time:
  30 minutes
Serves 4–6

½ cup self-raising flour	*8 thick, short sausages*
½ teaspoon salt	*50 g dripping*
2 eggs, lightly beaten	*1 small onion, thinly sliced*
1 cup milk	*1 cup plain flour*

1 Preheat oven to moderately hot 210°C (190°C gas). To make batter, sift flours and salt into a large jug. Make a well in the centre. Add combined eggs and milk gradually; whisk until smooth. Set aside for 15 minutes.
2 Prick sausages all over with a fork. Place half the dripping in a shallow 6-cup capacity ovenproof dish. Place dish in oven to heat while preparing sausages. Heat remaining dripping in a large frying pan and cook the sausages for 5 minutes until well browned. Transfer to a plate; add onions to pan and cook for 3 minutes, until soft.

3 Arrange sausages and onion in the heated dish.
4 Quickly pour batter over sausages and return to oven for 30 minutes until batter is set and golden. Serve immediately with mustard.
Note: Toad in the Hole was originally made with pieces of meat, instead of sausages. The meat was sometimes leftovers, giving it the reputation of being a frugal dish.
For a full flavour, use a good pork sausage. As an alternative, try one of the spiced sausages from specialist shops or your butcher.

Add combined milk and eggs gradually to sifted flour and salt.

Add onions to pan and cook until soft and golden.

Place sausages in bottom of heated
ovenproof dish.

Pour batter over sausages and bake until
batter is set and golden.

Yorkshire Fish Pie

Oatmeal makes an unusual pastry.

Preparation time:
10 minutes
+ 10 minutes
standing
Total cooking time:
30 minutes
Serves 4

750 g boneless white fish fillets, cut into 2 cm cubes **1/4 cup milk** **30 g butter** **salt to taste** **2 teaspoons finely grated lemon rind** **3 rashers bacon (rind removed)** **4 hard-boiled eggs, finely chopped**	**PASTRY TOPPING** **1 1/4 cups plain flour** **1/2 cup fine oatmeal** **100 g butter, chopped** **pinch salt** **water and lemon juice to moisten** **lightly beaten egg for glaze**

1 Preheat oven to moderate 180°C. Brush a 23 cm pie plate with melted butter or oil. In a large frying pan place fish fillets, milk, butter, salt and lemon rind; simmer, covered for 8 minutes. Remove from heat.
2 Grill bacon until crisp and chop finely. Add bacon and eggs to fish and pour into prepared pie plate.
3 To make Pastry: Combine flour, oatmeal, butter and salt in food processor. Using pulse action, press button for 30 seconds until mixture is fine and crumbly. Add water and lemon juice to bring to a dough. Remove, chill for 10 minutes before rolling out.
4 Roll out pastry, between two sheets of baking paper, to cover top of pie. Moisten edge of pie plate with egg, cover fish filling with pastry. Brush with egg and bake for 30 minutes.

Cut fish fillets into 2 cm cubes before cooking.

Combine grilled bacon, chopped eggs and fish.

Combine flour, oatmeal, butter and salt in food processor.

Brush edge of pie plate with egg, top with pastry.

41

Shepherd's Pie

A family favourite.

Preparation time:
  15 minutes
Total cooking time:
  1 hour
Serves 6

---

750 g lean cooked
  roast lamb
25 g dripping or
  butter
2 medium brown
  onions, thinly sliced
1/4 cup plain flour
1/2 teaspoon dry
  mustard
1 1/2 cups chicken
  stock
1/4 cup chopped
  fresh mint
1/4 cup chopped fresh
  parsley

1/2 teaspoon ground
  pepper
salt to taste
2 tablespoons
  worcestershire
  sauce

POTATO TOPPING
4 large old potatoes,
  cooked and mashed
1/4–1/3 cup hot milk
30 g butter
salt and pepper to
  taste

---

1 Brush an 8-cup capacity casserole with melted butter or oil. Preheat oven to moderately hot 210°C (190°C gas). Trim meat and cut into small cubes or mince. Melt dripping or butter in a large pan. Add onions and cook until golden.

2 Sprinkle in flour and mustard. Gradually add stock and blend, stirring, until smooth. Bring gravy to boil, reduce heat, simmer for 3 minutes.

3 Stir through meat, mint, parsley, pepper, salt and sauce. Remove from heat and spoon into dish.

4 To make Topping: Combine potato, milk, butter, salt and pepper. Mix until smooth and creamy. Spread evenly over meat; rough up surface with fork. Bake 40–45 minutes until heated through and potato topping is golden brown.

Trim cooked lamb and cut into small cubes.

Gradually add stock to onions and flour, stir till smooth.

Stir in meat, mint, parsley, pepper and worcestershire sauce.

Rough up the potato topping evenly with a fork.

Cornish Pasties

Lunchtime special.

Preparation time:
  30 minutes
Total cooking time:
  30 minutes
Makes 6 pasties

SHORTCRUST PASTRY
2½ cups plain flour
½ teaspoon dry
  mustard
120 g butter, chopped
1–3 tablespoons water

FILLING
250 g round or blade
  steak, finely
  chopped
2 small old potatoes,
  peeled and
  finely chopped

1 medium brown
  onion, peeled and
  finely chopped
¼ cup chopped fresh
  parsley
¼ cup beef or chicken
  stock
white pepper
salt to taste
¼ teaspoon English
  mustard
1 teaspoon grated
  horseradish
beaten egg to glaze

---

1 Preheat oven to moderately hot 210°C (190°C gas). Brush a baking tray with melted butter or oil. Place flour and mustard in food processor bowl, add butter. Using pulse action, process until mixture is fine and crumbly. Add almost all the water. Process 20 seconds or until mixture comes together, adding more water if necessary. Wrap in plastic wrap and refrigerate.

2 To prepare Filling: Combine steak, potatoes, onion and parsley. Add stock and season with pepper, salt, mustard and horseradish. Mix well.

3 Roll pastry out to 3 mm thickness. Cut out six circles, 16 cm in diameter, using a saucer as a guide. Divide the combined filling between the six circles, placing it into the centre of each circle.

4 Glaze the edge of the circle with egg and bring two sides together to form a half circle. With fingers, pinch to form a frill. Brush with egg and place on a baking tray in preheated oven for 10 minutes. Reduce heat to moderate 180°C and cook for further 20 minutes. Serve hot.

Note: Cold pasties are excellent for work or school lunches. They were originally baked for farmers who worked outside all day, and for miners. Family members would have their own preferences for fillings, and each pasty would be marked with its owner's initials. The pasty has the frill so that it can easily be held to eat.

Process flour, mustard and butter until mixture is fine and crumbly.

For filling, mix steak, potatoes, onion and parsley. Add stock and seasonings.

Divide filling among six circles of pastry, placing in centre of each.

Using fingers, pinch pastry edges to form a frill.

45

Peel and thinly slice potatoes and onions, chop bacon.

Cook bacon for 3 minutes, remove from pan and drain on paper towel.

VEGETABLES

English vegetable dishes are simple and delicious, the perfect accompaniment for grilled meat or a roast.

Pan Haggerty (Potato Cake with Crisp Topping)

Preparation time:
15 minutes
Total cooking time:
1–1½ hours
Serves 6–8

3 large old potatoes, peeled and thinly sliced	*3 medium onions, thinly sliced*
2 rashers bacon, rind removed and chopped	*30 g dripping*
	1¼ cups grated cheddar cheese
	white pepper, salt to taste

1 Melt dripping in a small pan, add bacon and cook 3 minutes, remove. Drain on paper towel.

2 Add onions and cook 5 minutes; remove.

3 Over the base of a heavy-based skillet or pan place one-third of the potato slices, overlapping each other. Sprinkle with one-third onion, one-third bacon and one-third cheese. Season with salt and pepper. Repeat with the remaining ingredients to form three layers of potato.

3 Cover with foil and cook over a low heat for 1 hour or until potatoes are tender when tested.

Note. The frying pan needs to have a solid base or the potatoes will burn and cook unevenly. Pan Haggerty can be cooked in a greased 23 cm cake tin in a moderate 180°C oven for 1–1½ hours.

Arrange one-third potatoes in pan, sprinkle with one-third onion and bacon.

Test potatoes with a knife to see if they are cooked.

47

Pease Pudding

Serve with ham or boiled beef.

Preparation time:
Overnight soaking
+ 10 minutes
Total cooking time:
2 hours
Serves 4

500 g split peas, soaked overnight and drained *1 onion, finely chopped* *1 sprig fresh rosemary*	*2 eggs, lightly beaten* *30 g butter, softened* *1/2 teaspoon white pepper* *salt to taste* *2 tablespoons malt vinegar*

1 Brush a 4-cup capacity ovenproof dish with melted butter or oil.
2 Place peas, onion and rosemary sprig into a large pan. Cover peas with water. Place lid on saucepan and cook over a gentle heat 1 hour or until the peas are starting to split.
3 Drain peas in a strainer or colander. Discard rosemary. Mash peas with potato masher. Add eggs, butter, pepper, salt and vinegar. Blend until smooth.
4 Preheat oven to moderate 180°C.

Pour pudding mixture into dish and stand in a bain marie. Bake for 30–45 minutes or until pudding sets. Unmould to serve. Alternatively, pour into 1.5 litre pudding steamer and steam for 1 hour.
Note: A bain marie is a pan of hot water – usually a baking dish – in which puddings and custards are cooked. This method ensures slow, even cooking of delicate foods.

HINT
For a delicious snack, try some leftover cold Pease Pudding spread on a chunk of bread and topped with thin slices of ham.

Brush a 4-cup capacity ovenproof dish with melted butter.

Place rosemary sprig in pan with soaked split peas and chopped onion.

Add eggs, butter, pepper, salt and vinegar to mashed pea mixture.

Place dish in baking dish; pour in water to come halfway up sides.

Baked Onions

Good with a roast.

Preparation time:
15 minutes
Total cooking time:
35 minutes
Serves 6

6 medium brown
  onions
2 rashers bacon, rind
  removed, chopped
1 cup soft white
  breadcrumbs
1/2 teaspoon dried
  sage

2 tablespoons sherry
1 tablespoon chopped
  fresh parsley
1/2 teaspoon ground
  black pepper
salt to taste
1/2 teaspoon ground
  mace

1 Preheat oven to
moderate 180°C. Cut
top quarter off onions
and peel; leave roots
attached to prevent
them falling apart
during cooking.
2 Simmer onions in
boiling water for
15 minutes. Remove,
drain well and cool.
3 In a bowl, combine
bacon, breadcrumbs,
sage, sherry, parsley,
pepper, salt and mace.
4 Remove centre third
from onion to form a
hollow for the filling;
finely chop the
removed onion and
add to filling. Pile
filling into cavity,
place in baking dish
and bake 20 minutes.

Cut top quarter off onions and peel; leave root attached.

Remove cooked onions from pan and drain well; allow to cool.

50

Combine bacon, breadcrumbs, sage, sherry, parsley, salt and pepper.

Spoon filling into onion cavities; bake for 20 minutes.

51

Braised Celery

A rich side dish.

Preparation time:
15 minutes
Total cooking time:
40 minutes
Serves 6

---

1 head celery
30 g butter
2 cups chicken stock
2 teaspoons finely
  grated lemon rind
1/4 cup lemon juice
1/4 cup cream
2 egg yolks

1 tablespoon
  cornflour
1/4 cup chopped
  parsley
white pepper
salt to taste
1/2 teaspoon ground
  mace

---

1 Lightly brush a
6-cup capacity
shallow heatproof
dish with melted
butter or oil. Preheat
oven to moderate
180°C. Trim celery
and cut into 5 cm
lengths. Melt butter
in a large pan. Add
celery, toss to coat
evenly in butter.

Cover with a lid and
cook for 2 minutes.
2 Pour over stock,
lemon rind and juice;
cover and simmer for
10 minutes. Remove
celery with a slotted
spoon and place into
prepared dish.
Remove two cups of
cooking liquid.
3 Blend cream, egg

yolks and cornflour
together. Whisk in
cooking liquid.
Return to heat and
cook until mixture
boils and thickens,
add parsley, pepper,
salt and mace.
4 Pour sauce over
celery in heatproof
dish. Cook in oven
15–20 minutes or
until celery softens.
Note: Celery
sometimes has a
slightly bitter flavour,
which is removed
by cooking.

HINT
To make an unusual
first course, cook the
celery as above, then
wrap several pieces
of celery in a slice of
ham. Pour the sauce
over to serve.

Trim head of celery and cut stalks into
5 cm lengths.

Removed cooked celery from pan with
slotted spoon.

Add parsley, pepper, salt and mace to thickened sauce mixture.

Pour sauce over celery in heatproof dish; bake 15-20 minutes.

Place overlapping slices of buttered bread into greased dish.

Mix eggs, cream, milk, essence and sugar; pour over sultanas and bread slices.

DESSERTS

These are the tried and true favourites, like Apple Crumble, Trifle, and the irresistible Summer Pudding, made of berries.

Bread and Butter Pudding

Preparation time:
20 minutes
Total cooking time:
40–50 minutes
Serves 6–8

1/2 cup sultanas	*1/2 cup soft brown*
1/4 cup brandy	*sugar*
30 g butter	*2 tablespoons*
10 slices white bread	*demerara sugar*
3 eggs, lightly beaten	*1/2 teaspoon ground*
1 1/4 cups cream	*cinnamon*
1 1/4 cups milk	
1 teaspoon vanilla	
essence	

1 Grease 4 cm-deep 6–cup capacity heatproof dish with melted butter or oil. Preheat oven to moderate 180°C.

Soak sultanas in brandy until all brandy is absorbed. Spread bread slices with butter and cut into halves. Place overlapping slices decoratively into prepared dish.

2 Scatter sultanas over bread. Whisk together eggs, cream, milk, essence and soft brown sugar. Pour egg mixture onto bread. Stand for 10 minutes before baking.

3 Sprinkle demerara sugar and cinnamon over, cover with aluminium foil, bake 20 minutes. Remove foil, cook a further 20 minutes or until set. Serve pudding with whipped cream and fruit.

Sprinkle top evenly with demerara sugar, then with cinnamon.

Remove foil and cook a further 20 minutes or until pudding is set.

55

Trifle

An irresistible combination of flavours and textures.

Preparation time:
20 minutes
+ 50 minutes
refrigeration
Total cooking time:
10 minutes
Serves 6–8

---

*1 sponge cake,
  16 cm diameter
  x 3 cm deep*
*2/3 cup cream sherry
  or port*
3/4 cup boiling water
*85 g packet red jelly
  crystals*
2/3 cup cold water
1/4 cup sugar
1/4 cup custard powder

2 1/2 cups milk
*1 teaspoon vanilla
  essence*
1 egg
*2 x 425 g cans peach
  slices, drained*
1 cup cream
1/4 cup icing sugar
*250 g punnet
  strawberries*

---

1 Cut sponge into 2 cm cubes and place in an 8-cup capacity serving dish. Drizzle sherry over the cake.
2 Pour boiling water over jelly crystals and stir until dissolved. Add cold water. Pour into a 28 x 18 cm tin and refrigerate 30 minutes or until set.
3 Place sugar and custard powder into a medium pan, gradually blend in milk. Stir over medium heat with a wooden spoon until custard boils and thickens. Remove from heat. Add essence and egg, mix well. Cover surface with plastic wrap, cool to room temperature.
4 Using a plastic spatula, cut jelly into cubes. Place in a layer on top of sponge. Add fruit for the next layer, then pour custard over top. Refrigerate for 20 minutes or until custard has set. Whip cream with icing sugar until thick, pipe or spoon decoratively onto trifle and garnish with strawberries.

Cut cake into 2 cm cubes and drizzle sherry over.

Dissolve jelly crystals in boiling water; pour in cold water.

Stir custard over medium heat until it boils and thickens.

When jelly is set, cut into cubes with a plastic spatula.

Apple Crumble

Eat hot or cold.

Preparation time:
  30 minutes
Total cooking time:
  25–30 minutes
Serves 4–6

---

4 large green cooking apples, peeled and sliced
1 tablespoon soft brown sugar
2 tablespoons golden syrup
2 tablespoons lemon juice

TOPPING
³/4 cup self-raising flour
1/2 cup desiccated coconut
1/2 cup rolled oats
1/2 cup soft brown sugar
100 g butter

---

1 Preheat oven to moderate 180°C. Brush a shallow 6-cup capacity casserole dish with melted butter or oil. Place apples, sugar, golden syrup and lemon juice in a large pan; cover with tight-fitting lid and cook over a low heat for 10 minutes or until apples soften.
2 Spoon apple mixture into dish.
3 In a bowl combine flour, coconut, rolled oats and sugar; mix well. Make a well in the centre. Melt butter and pour into bowl with dry ingredients. Mix to form a crumble.
4 Scatter crumble mixture over apples. Bake for 25–30 minutes or until top is crisp and golden. Serve with whipped cream or ice-cream.

HINT
For a subtle difference in flavour, add 50 g ginger in syrup. Chop the ginger pieces finely, and cook with the apples.
Pears or a bunch of rhubarb may be substituted for the apples. Rhubarb has a sour flavour, so increase the soft brown sugar from one tablespoonful to two.

Peel and slice apples and place in pan. Add sugar, syrup and lemon juice.

Spoon cooked apple mixture into greased casserole dish.

Mix dry ingredients, make well in centre and pour in melted butter.

Scatter crumble mixture over apples and bake until crisp and golden.

59

Summer Pudding

Prepare the day before serving.

Preparation time:
20 minutes
Total cooking time:
8 minutes +
overnight
refrigeration
Serves 6

---

200 g red currants, stalks removed
200 g strawberries, hulled

¾ cup sugar
200 g raspberries
9 slices day-old white toasting bread

---

1 Place red currants and strawberries in a large pan, sprinkle with sugar. Stir gently over a low heat for 5 minutes, until the sugar dissolves in the fruit juices.

2 Add raspberries and cook for a further 3 minutes, stirring occasionally, until fruit has softened. Remove from heat and allow to cool.

3 Remove crusts from bread. Cut a round from one slice of bread to cover the base of a 4-cup capacity bowl; line the sides with bread slices, overlapping them slightly.

4 Pour the fruit mixture into bread-lined bowl. Top with bread slices trimmed to cover surface. Cover with plastic wrap, place a small saucer onto the plastic. Place a weight, such as a can, onto the saucer and refrigerate overnight. To serve, invert pudding onto a serving plate and cut it into wedges. Serve with plenty of thick cream, to balance the strong flavour of the fruit. **Note:** The bread must not be too fresh or it will not absorb the juices of the fruits. Frozen strawberries and raspberries may be used, if fresh are not available, or blackberries or blackcurrants could be used instead.

Sprinkle red currants and strawberries with sugar.

Add raspberries and cook 3 minutes until fruit has softened.

.ine sides of bowl with bread slices, overlapping slightly.

Place a weight on saucer, refrigerate pudding overnight.

Spotted Dick

A fruity pudding.

Preparation time:
15 minutes
Total cooking time:
35 minutes
Serves 4

---

1 1/3 cups plain flour
1 1/2 teaspoons baking
    powder
1/2 cup sugar
1 1/2 teaspoons
    ground ginger
2 cups soft
    breadcrumbs
1/2 cup sultanas
3/4 cup currants

1 1/2 cups (120 g)
    shredded suet
2 teaspoons finely
    grated lemon rind
2 eggs, lightly beaten
1 cup milk

custard or cream to
serve

---

1 Brush a 1.5-litre capacity pudding steamer with melted butter or oil. Line base with baking paper, grease paper. Grease a large sheet of aluminium foil and a large sheet of greaseproof paper. Lay the paper over the foil, greased side up, and pleat it in the centre. Sift flour, baking powder, sugar and ginger into a large bowl. Add breadcrumbs, sultanas and currants, suet and rind. Mix well with a wooden spoon.

2 Combine egg and milk, add to dry ingredients, mix well. Spoon mixture into prepared pudding steamer. Cover with greased foil and paper, greased side down. Place lid over foil, bring clips up and secure firmly with string.

3 If you have no lid, lay a pleated tea-towel over the foil and tie it securely with string under the lip of the basin. Knot the four ends of the tea-towel together, forming a handle to lower the basin into the pan.

4 Place the basin in a large, deep pan. Carefully pour boiling water down the side of the pan to come halfway up the side of the basin. Bring to the boil, cover and cook for 2½ hours. Do not let the pudding boil dry. Replenish with boiling water as the pudding cooks. Unmould pudding onto serving plate, cut into slices and serve with warm custard or cream.

HINT
Custard may be made the traditional way, with eggs, caster sugar, milk and cornflour cooked over a double boiler or in a bain marie. If you prefer to use custard powder, give it extra flavour by adding some nutmeg, a twist of lemon peel, or a tablespoon of brandy to replace some of the milk.

Lay paper over greased foil and make a pleat in the centre.

Combine egg and milk and add to dry ingredients; mix well.

If using a tea-towel, tie with string under lip of the basin.

Carefully pour boiling water down the side of the pan.

INDEX